GETTING TO KNOW THE WORLD'S GREATEST ARTISTS

E D G A R
DEGAS

WRITTEN AND ILLUSTRATED BY MIKE VENEZIA

CHILDREN'S PRESS®
A DIVISION OF GROLIER PUBLISHING
NEW YORK   LONDON   HONG KONG   SYDNEY
DANBURY, CONNECTICUT

For Steve Wolowina, one of the best people I can bounce art ideas off of—thanks for your help and inspiration.

Cover: *Ballet at the Paris Opera,* by Edgar Degas. 1876-77. Pastel over monotype on ivory paper. 35.9 x 71.9 cm. Gift of Mary and Leigh B. Block, 1981.12. © Art Institute of Chicago.

Colorist for illustrations: Kathy Hickey

Library of Congress Cataloging-in-Publication Data

Venezia, Mike.
    Edgar Degas / written and illustrated by Mike Venezia.
      p. cm. — (Getting to know the world's greatest artists)
    Summary: Examines the life and work of the nineteenth-century artist Edgar Degas, who loved to paint scenes of Paris and the people who worked and lived there.
    ISBN 0-516-21593-0 (lib.bdg.)   0-516-27172-5 (pbk.)
    1. Degas, Edgar, 1834-1917—Juvenile literature. 2. Painters—France—Biography—Juvenile literature. [1. Degas, Edgar, 1834-1917. 2. Artists. 3. Painting, French. 4. Art appreciation.] I. Title.
ND553.D3 V46 2000
709'.2-dc21
[B]   99-058035
                                     CIP
                                     AC

Self-Portrait, by Edgar Degas. 1863. Oil on canvas. 92.5 x 66.5 cm. Museu Calouste Gulbenkian, Lisbon, Portugal. Photograph © Giraudon/BAL36822 © Bridgeman Art Library International Ltd., London/New York.

Edgar Degas was born in Paris, France, in 1834. During the 1800s, Paris was the art center of the world, so it was a good place to be if you were interested in becoming an artist. While growing up, Edgar was able to see great works of art from the past as well as drawings and paintings done by modern artists.

The Parade, or Race Horses in front of the Stands, by Edgar Degas. 1866-68. Oil on paper laid on canvas. 46 x 61 cm. Musée d'Orsay, Paris, France. © Reunion des Musées Nationaux/USA99561 © Bridgeman Art Library International Ltd., London/New York.

Ironing Women, by Edgar Degas. Oil on canvas. Photograph by H. Lewandowski. © Photo RMN.

Some of Edgar Degas's most famous works of art are scenes of Paris and the people who worked and lived there.

Degas loved painting, drawing, and making pastel pictures of the racetrack, washerwomen, and café singers.

The Rehearsal, by Edgar Degas. 1877. Oil on canvas. 58.4 x 83.8 cm. Burrell Collection, Glasgow, Scotland. BAL2965 © Bridgeman Art Library International Ltd., London/New York.

One of Edgar Degas's all-time favorite subjects was the ballet. He loved to show ballerinas rehearsing backstage. He showed dancers warming up, stretching, talking to each other, and practicing their movements, which gave these paintings a very real and natural look.

Danseuse au Bouquet, by Edgar Degas. Pastel over monotype. 15 7/8 x 19 7/8 in. Gift of Mrs. Murray S. Danforth. © Museum of Art, Rhode Island School of Design.

Ballet Rehearsal on the Stage, by Edgar Degas. 1874. Oil on canvas. 65 x 81 cm. Musée d'Orsay, Paris, France. Photograph © Bulloz/ BUZ16631 © Bridgeman Art Library International Ltd., London/New York.

Edgar Degas grew up in a wealthy family. His father owned and operated a large bank. Fortunately for Edgar, Mr. Degas liked art and music a lot more than running a bank. He often took his son to art museums and galleries in Paris.

Madonna of the Rocks, by Leonardo da Vinci. 1483. Oil on canvas. 199 x 122 cm. Louvre, Paris, France. Photograph by Erich Lessing. © Art Resource, NY.

It was during this time that Edgar became interested in art. He was fascinated with the paintings of great Old Master Renaissance artists like Raphael, Leonardo da Vinci, and Andrea Mantegna.

Calvary, by Andrea Mantegna. Central panel of the predella from the San Zeno altarpiece in Verona, ordered by the protonotary Gregorio Correr. Wood. 76 x 96 cm. Louvre, Paris, France. Photograph by Erich Lessing. © Art Resource, NY.

After Edgar Degas finished high school, his father decided Edgar should study law. Mr. Degas hoped his son would help run the bank someday. Instead of going to his classes, though, Edgar spent most of his time studying and copying paintings at the Louvre. The Louvre was a famous art museum in Paris that

allowed students to copy great works of art.

During his studies, Edgar learned there were two popular but very different styles of art. Artists had serious arguments and took sides about which style they thought was the best. One was called Neoclassical and the other was called Romantic.

Mme. Recamier, by Jacques Louis David. Louvre, Paris, France. © Art Resource, NY/Scala.

Neoclassical artists, such as Jacques Louis David and Jean Auguste Ingres, thought paintings should have a calm, orderly feeling. They believed drawing and painting with line was the best way to do this. Neoclassical artists used very few bright colors, and you can barely see their brush strokes.

Romantic artists, like Theodore Géricault and Eugene Delacroix, were completely different. They worked hard to put feelings into their paintings. They liked scenes of exciting battles and the fury of nature. Romantic artists used quick brush strokes and more color to get their feelings across.

The Combat of the Giaour and Hassan, by Eugène Delacroix. 1826. Oil on canvas. 59.6 x 73.4 cm. Gift of Mrs. Bertha Palmer Thorne, Mrs. Rose Movius Palmer, and Mr. and Mrs. Arthur M. Wood, 1962.966. © Art Institute of Chicago.

Degas thought there were good things about both the Neoclassical and Romantic styles. He couldn't wait to try ideas from each in his own paintings. When Edgar finally decided to tell his father that he would much rather be an artist than a lawyer, his father accepted his decision. Edgar started out by going to the best art schools in Paris.

Edgar soon felt, however, that he could learn better on his own. In 1856, when he was twenty-two years old, Edgar Degas took a trip to Italy to study the great Italian artists. He learned a lot and gained confidence there. Near the end of his trip, he began a large painting of his Italian relatives.

The Bellelli Family, by Edgar Degas. 1858-67. Oil on canvas. Musée d'Orsay, Paris, France. QED28949
© Bridgeman Art Library International Ltd., London/New York.

Degas was very excited about this portrait. Since it was too large to finish in the small room he was staying in, Edgar hurried back to Paris, where he had more space to work.

Marguerite Degas, by Edgar Degas. 1858-60.
Oil on canvas. Musée d'Orsay. Photograph by
Gerard Blot. © Photo RMN.

Rene Degas, by Edgar Degas. 1855. Oil on canvas.
36 1/2 x 29 1/2 in. Purchased, Drayton Hillyer
Fund, 1935. © Smith College Museum of Art,
Northampton, Massachusetts.

When Edgar Degas returned home to
Paris, he set up a studio and continued work
on *The Bellelli Family,* as well as on portraits
of his own family. He started doing historical
scenes, too. In Paris, Edgar met lots of other
artists his own age. He enjoyed having
discussions about art with them.

One of Degas's artist friends, Édouard Manet, suggested that Edgar enter his paintings in the biggest art show in Paris. It was called the Salon. People who were interested in buying artwork came from all over the world to see the paintings displayed there.

The Daughter of Jephthah, by Edgar Degas. 1859-60. Oil on canvas. 77 x 117 1/2 in. Purchased, Drayton Hillyer Fund, 1933. © Smith College Museum of Art, Northampton, Massachusetts.

Unlike the rest of his friends, Edgar Degas didn't have to worry about selling his paintings, since he had plenty of money. But he did want his artwork to get noticed. Edgar entered his paintings in the Salon, and some of them were accepted. His dark, carefully painted history scenes and portraits were just what the Salon judges wanted.

Unfortunately, no one else seemed to pay any attention to his paintings. Even if an artist's work was accepted by the Salon, that artist still might be disappointed. Paintings were often hung so high up on the wall that hardly anyone could see them!

A Woman Seated Beside a Vase of Flowers, by Edgar Degas. 1865. Oil on canvas. 29 x 36 1/2 in. H. O. Havemeyer Collection, Bequest of Mrs. H. O. Havemeyer, 1929. © The Metropolitan Museum of Art/Photograph © 1998.

Edgar never really liked the Salon. There were too many rules and the judges were snobby. Edgar Degas was trying out some new ideas now. He started painting scenes of everyday events, and added more color to his work. These were paintings that the Salon judges would probably never accept.

Sadly, at this time, Edgar's father died. After he died, it was discovered that he hadn't been a very good bank manager. Mr. Degas owed people lots of money, and Edgar had to pay them back. Soon there wasn't much left of the Degas family fortune.

For the first time ever, Edgar Degas needed to sell his paintings. Fortunately, some of his artist friends decided to put on their own show. Edgar jumped at the chance to join them.

The Opera Orchestra, by Edgar Degas. 1870. Oil on canvas. 56.5 x 46 cm. Musée d'Orsay, Paris, France. BAL16124 © Bridgeman Art Library International Ltd., London/New York.

Stacks of Wheat (End of Summer), by Claude Monet. 1890-91. Oil on canvas. 60 x 100 cm. Gift of Arthur M. Wood, in memory of Pauline Palmer Wood, 1985.1103. © Art Institute of Chicago.

Edgar didn't know it at the time, but he and his friends would become one of the best-known groups of artists ever. Edgar Degas, Claude Monet, Alfred Sisley, Camille Pissarro, and Pierre Auguste Renoir would soon be known as the Impressionists.

The Road in the Woods, by Alfred Sisley. 1879. Canvas, oil on linen. 18 1/4 x 22 in. The Chester Dale Collection. Photograph by Richard Carafelli. ©National Gallery of Art, Washington, DC.

The Luncheon of the Boating Party, by Pierre Auguste Renoir. 1881. Oil on canvas. 51 x 68 in. Acquired 1923. © The Phillips Collection, Washington, DC.

The Impressionists tried new ideas in art that had never been seen before. They liked to paint natural scenes of everyday life. They were interested in showing the way sunlight looked when it fell on a haystack or on a tree or on people. The Impressionists painted their scenes outdoors on the spot, using quick, loose brush strokes to capture a moment in time.

The Impressionists' first show didn't go over very well. No one understood their new ideas. In fact, people hated most of the paintings they saw. They thought the paintings looked unfinished and out of focus.

At the Races in the Countryside, by Edgar Degas. 1869. Oil on canvas. 14 3/8 x 22 in. © 1931 Purchase Fund. Courtesy, Museum of Fine Arts, Boston.

Edgar Degas was one of the few artists who had any luck. He sold seven of the ten paintings he had entered in the show. *At the Races in the Countryside* was one of the paintings Edgar exhibited. People found it easier to accept Degas' well-drawn, carefully painted figures than the paintings of the other artists.

A Woman Ironing, by Edgar Degas. 1874. Oil on canvas. 21 3/8 x 15 1/2 in. H. O. Havemeyer Collection, Bequest of Mrs. H. O. Havemeyer, 1929. © The Metropolitan Museum of Art/Photograph © 1994.

Although Edgar Degas was a member of the Impressionist group and even became one of their leaders, his work was very different from his friends' paintings. Edgar enjoyed painting scenes of people in natural poses like the other Impressionists, but that was about the only thing he had in common with them.

The Dance Class, by Edgar Degas. 1874. Oil on canvas. 32 3/4 x 30 1/4 in. Bequest of Mrs. Harry Payne Bingham, 1986. © The Metropolitan Museum of Art/ Photograph © 1987.

Degas couldn't stand the thought of painting outdoors, capturing a moment in time. He preferred making lots of sketches to bring back to his studio where he could work alone, thoughtfully arranging his subjects and lighting them the way he liked.

As time went on, Edgar Degas became a very successful artist. People loved his paintings and pastels. Later in life, Edgar became interested in photography.

The Millinery Shop, by Edgar Degas. 1884-90. Oil on canvas. 100 x 110 cm. Mr. and Mrs. Lewis Larned Coburn Memorial Collection, 1933.428. © The Art Institute of Chicago.